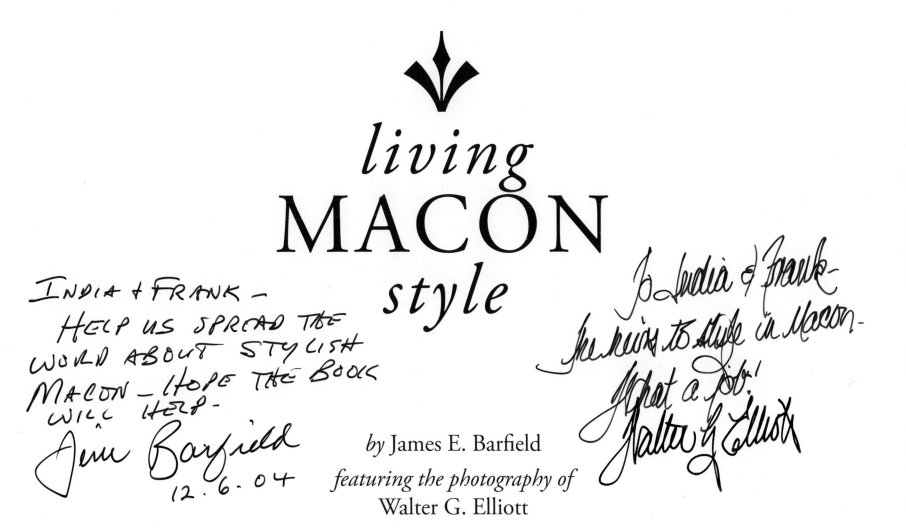

living
MACON
style

by James E. Barfield

featuring the photography of
Walter G. Elliott

INDIA + FRANK —
HELP US SPREAD THE
WORD ABOUT STYLISH
MACON — HOPE THE BOOK
WILL HELP —
Jim Barfield
12.6.04

To India + Frank —
the keys to style in Macon —
What a Job!
Walter G. Elliott

Henchard Press, Ltd.

Publisher	Henry S. Beers
Editor-in-Chief	Martha Elrod
Art Director/Designer	Jennifer Shermer Pack
Assistant Designer	Julianne Gleaton
Operations Manager	Gary Pulliam
Associate Publisher	Richard J. Hutto

Cover photography by Walter G. Elliott.
Front cover is the staircase from the Elliott house. Back cover is the loggia of the Thornsberry house.

All photography by Walter G. Elliott, except for black and white photos on pages 32 and 72.

Edited to *The Chicago Manual of Style*
© 2004 by Henchard Press, Ltd.

Printed in Korea

Library of Congress Control Number: 2004115427

ISBN: 0-9762875-0-1

Henchard Press books are available at quantity discounts
with bulk purchase for educational, business, or sales promotional use.
For information, please write to:
Henchard Press, Ltd., 3920 Ridge Avenue, Macon, GA 31210, or call 866-311-9578.

Acknowledgements

Mr. and Mrs. Alpha M. Bond, Jr.

Mr. and Mrs. John D. Comer

Mr. and Mrs. Lovick P. Corn

Mrs. Elizabeth Hay Curtis

Eugene C. Dunwody, Jr.

Mr. and Mrs. J. Sewell Elliott

Mssrs. Sewell, Frank, Randy and Bruce Elliott

Dr. R. Kirby Godsey

Mrs. Sara Jackson Hertwig

Dr. and Mrs. Peter O. Holliday, III

Mr. and Mrs. Richard J. Hutto

Mr. and Mrs. Frank C. Jones

Mr. and Mrs. John F. Rogers, Jr.

Trudie and Brandt Sessions

Mrs. Phil J. Sheradan

Mr. and Mrs. Tim Sheridan

Mr. and Mrs. E. Raymond Smith

Mr. and Mrs. Robert A. Smith

Dr. Stella I. Tsai

Mr. John W. Waldvogel

Mrs. Gloria McAfee Wynn

Table of Contents

Foreword			7
Introduction			8
Sams	4569 Rivoli Drive	1829	10
Oliver	1183 Georgia Avenue	1848	14
Holliday	607 College Street	1854	20
Reichert	920 High Street	1857	28
Battin	348 College Street	1886	32
Cerny	1085 Georgia Avenue	1887	36
Faircloth	3395 Osborne Place	1900	42
Barfield	1962 Forsyth Street	1908	50
Whitten	340 College Street	1908	54
Walden	1238 Jefferson Terrace	1911	60
Comer	2590 Vineville Avenue	1923	66
Rader	3557 Vineville Avenue	1923	72
Chapman	1158 Oakcliff Road	1927	78
Curtis	150 Tucker Road	1927	86
Hogan	114 Cleveland Avenue	1928	94
Thornsberry	2694 Stanislaus Circle	1929	100
McCleary	1790 Waverland Drive	1941	108
Fickling	2929 Ingleside Avenue	1949	112
Sheridan	2727 Ingleside Avenue	1950	116
Waldvogel	1855 Twin Pines Drive	1956	122
Rogers	280 Country Club Road	1957	130
Sessions	2691 Stanislaus Circle	1957	134
Elliott	480 Pierce Avenue	1960	140
Hertwig	1120 Oakcliff Road	1965	146
	Suburban Rivoli	1995	152

Foreword

Is there a Macon style? A strong case can be made that there is. To discover its essence, combine the Southerner's innate sense of place, love of the past, and attachment to family traditions with the Georgian's pride in a rich architectural heritage. Add some creativity, imagination, and an eye for beauty without ostentation. Season with the Maconite's bent for hospitality and an alluring tinge of eccentricity. The powerful mixture of these qualities or, more accurately, forces inspires dwelling places that are appealing to the eye, lovely to live in, and pleasurable to visit, offering comfort to resident and guest alike and, above all, that are interesting.

That a house be interesting is the essential criterion for its inclusion in this book. The twenty-five houses you are invited to visit in the following pages are all interesting. Some are historic, some are recent. Some are quite large, others modest in size. Some reflect traditional design concepts while others represent experimental departures. All share the Macon style of livable, unforced elegance and proper scale and proportion. All are outfitted with attention to detail, with suitable furnishings, art and objects, and all are set in an appropriate landscape of lawns and gardens.

All of these interesting Macon houses are also homes. A house may remain a house when used as a shop or an office or even when empty, but a home is where people live. People live in and love each of the homes featured here. Over time, as people live in their homes, their needs often change. So houses are often altered. Alterations should respect the spirit of the architecture, and in each of these houses architectural integrity has been maintained.

With each house the photographer has sought to capture the essence of Macon style. The writer has attempted to describe it. As you enjoy your visit to these twenty- five interesting houses make an effort to identify for yourself the elements of Macon style.

Sinuous curves, simple iron balusters, and rich wood of a rail that has known the hands of generations of a family combine in a staircase representing Macon style.

Introduction

Macon, Georgia is an old Southern town enriched by an abundance of fine residential architecture. Almost from its inception, Macon has been blessed with the works of talented architects or, as the early ones were called, master builders. We honor them by remembering their illustrious names, among whom were: Elam Alexander; James B. Ayres; David B. Woodruff; Curran Ellis; Alexander Blair; William Oliphant; Neel Reid; Elliott Dunwody, Jr.; the Dennis family; Ellamae Ellis League; Delmar Warren; and Bernard Webb. But, in fact, their best memorials are the buildings they designed, which stand as testaments to their talent. And many do still stand. Whether farsighted or simply fortunate, Macon has lost relatively few of its finest buildings. Our wide streets helped check the spread of devastating fires. Sherman's incendiaries passed us by. And that awesome destroyer of historic building, "progress," was not so ravenous here.

As early as 1830, travel writer Anne Royal described Macon as "the rosebud of all little cities." In 1874 author Bret Harte wrote that Macon houses were ". . . very beautifully equipped and have a certain broad ease and munificence." Almost a century later, in 1970, nationally recognized architectural critics Carl Feiss and Russell Wright, in their survey of the town's architecture, declared "The city of Macon is a treasury of great historic buildings. . . . The range of architectural wealth is almost limitless."

The town plan for Macon devised by engineer/surveyor James Webb in 1822 called for a grid system of wide streets meeting at right angles. Contrary to a longstanding local myth, Webb's plan bore little resemblance to the plan of ancient Babylon. The reasons for main streets being alternately 120 and 180 feet wide were fire safety and public health. Aesthetics were not the primary concern. The first houses built on the new streets were simple frame structures making use of the plentiful supply of timber available. But Macon grew rapidly and before the end of its first decade stylish houses of brick and stucco were being constructed.

The reason for Macon's rapid growth was the great demand for its basic commodity, cotton. The town's location on the Fall Line made it the farthest inland destination for river traffic. Farmers from the north and west brought their precious cotton to Macon to be sold and shipped down the Ocmulgee and Altamaha Rivers to the coast. In 1843 a rail line was completed linking Macon and Savannah and the town's distribution capabilities were multiplied. Following the War Between the States Macon's first cotton mills made it part of the New South. By the early twentieth century several local mills gave work to hundreds of Macon citizens. When demand for cotton was high the town prospered and periods of prosperity always brought booms in building.

It was in the town's second decade that residents began to build more elaborate houses on the heights above the flat river valley. New Greek Revival temples and Italianate villas began to embellish Beall's Hill and College Hill. It was in 1836 that Encampment Hill was chosen to be the site of the new Georgia Female College, the first in the world chartered to grant degrees to women. At that time the city government renamed the hill "College Hill". Two entrepreneurs, Jerry Cowles and Robert Collins, bought the land adjacent to the college site and there developed

Macon's first "suburb." They retained two choice lots for themselves and each built on his lot a splendid Greek Revival mansion. Cowles' house still stands and is now called Woodruff House by its owner, Mercer University. It was designed by Elam Alexander who is credited with also designing the original Greek Revival building for the Georgia Female College which, soon after it opened, was renamed Wesleyan College. College Hill became Macon's most fashionable address and remained so for over a century.

Even during the long bleak era of Reconstruction following the War Between the States, Macon continued to build. Small Victorian cottages and grand Queen Anne mansions all boast the gingerbread trim, stained glass windows, and exuberant ornamentation of the late nineteenth century. Early in the twentieth century the automobile made possible the expansion of Macon's residential areas into new suburbs such as Cherokee Heights, North Highlands, Ingleside, and Shirley Hills. The once separate village of Vineville was incorporated into Macon. Prosperity spawned hundreds of new suburban houses in new architectural styles including Craftsman-Bungalow, Beaux Arts, English Medieval, and Classic Revival. After World War II Macon's economy became more diversified, no longer dependent on cotton. The town continued to prosper and expand and architects designed practical tract houses to meet the demand for affordable housing. During the 1950s the split-level ranch house became the popular choice in Macon while the more adventurous homebuilders chose bold new contemporary designs now identified as Mid-Century Modern.

Early in the twenty-first century Macon's continuing outward expansion often carries homebuilders beyond the limits of the town and even the county. Their imaginative new house designs reflect the demands of modern lifestyles. Alternatively, an increasing number of people have discovered the pleasures of living in town, the charm of period architecture, and the benefits of historic preservation. And many of them are choosing to renovate or maintain houses in Macon's seven residential National Register Historic Districts.

Two organizations led the way toward recognizing and preserving the best of Macon's architecture. In 1964, the Middle Georgia Historical Society was formed and shortly thereafter organized a comprehensive survey of Macon's historic architecture. Among the best results of that survey was a book, *A Guide to Macon's Architectural and Historical Heritage*, which remains the standard work for those interested in the historic architecture of Macon. In 1973, the Society acquired and renovated for its use the cottage on High Street where the poet Sidney Lanier was born in 1842. Two years later the Intown Macon Neighborhood Association partnered with the Middle Georgia Historical Society to found a new preservation organization, the Macon Heritage Foundation. A revolving fund was created for the acquisition and protection of endangered properties. Over a period of twenty-eight years MHF rescued hundreds of buildings valued at millions of dollars. In partnership with the National Trust for Historic Preservation, and with assistance from Mercer University, the Foundation revitalized two entire neighborhoods, Huguenin Heights and Tattnall Square Heights. These projects have served as models for similar efforts nationwide.

With the slogan "unity for the community" and the conviction that "together we're better" the Middle Georgia Historical Society and the Macon Heritage Foundation were merged in August of 2003 to form the Historic Macon Foundation. With combined strength and renewed energy the new organization is fulfilling its mission of educating the Macon community about its history and historic preservation, of preserving and restoring historic places, and of maintaining and promoting the Sidney Lanier Cottage. In fulfillment of the education function of its stated mission, the Historic Macon Foundation is a partner in the production of this book.

*Originally sited on downtown Walnut Street, this perfect 1829
Greek Revival cottage now sits on a rise in suburban Rivoli.*

4569 Rivoli Drive
1829
Sams

In 1829 Macon was only six years old when Jerry Cowles, a young businessman relocating from Milledgeville, commissioned master builder Elam Alexander to design for him and his family a new house on prestigious Walnut Street. Alexander chose the fashionable Greek Revival style for the Cowles' story and a half stucco cottage with an ionic portico. And so was created one of America's most admired cottages, a design emulated many times in Macon and around the country. Both Cowles' family and fortune grew and, after only six years, he had Alexander design and build for him a much larger Greek Revival house. That house, now known as Woodruff House and owned by Mercer University, still crowns the hill overlooking downtown Macon.

In 1948 Cowles' classic cottage was threatened with demolition by a department store, which needed its space for parking. A spirited young couple, Betty and Alfred Sams, decided to save the house by dismantling it and reconstructing it several miles away at suburban Rivoli. Betty Sams' uncle, the talented architect Elliott Dunwody, Jr., served as adviser on the reconstruction of the cottage on its new site at the crest of a gentle slope rising from Rivoli Drive. Credit for its success also belongs to the contractor, Louis Davidson, who, with passionate dedication, helped supervise this complicated and difficult project—marking countless pieces of the structure and organizing them for re-assembly. The happy results of the collaboration of homeowners, architect, and contractor was the preservation in context of the moldings, medallions, mantels, columns, windows, and doors belonging to an exceptional piece of architecture and history. Those who observe the sophistication and quality of the woodcarving and plasterwork are surprised that such skilled craftsmen were available in 1830 Macon—a town only recently carved from the wilderness.

For almost sixty years the Sams have enjoyed their house, reared their children in it, and lovingly cared for it. Today the house is filled with exactly the right furnishings befitting its age and style. Many are inherited family pieces while others are discoveries of the Sams, ardent and educated antique hunters. After experiencing this authentic combination of early architecture and period furnishings a visitor leaves the Sams house with the sensation of having been privileged to visit the Macon of long ago.

Above, The Sams' extraordinary collection of antiques fits beautifully in the 1829 rooms, as here in the parlor.

Upper right, Portraits of Betty and Alfred Sams, who deserve accolades for saving this architectureal treasure, hang in the parlor and dining room.

Below right, A graceful arch breaks the hall that runs through the center of the house. Meticulous care was taken to preserve windows, doors, floors, moldings, and medallions when the house was moved.

The Sams' kitchen is located in an original wing of the house. They added a matching wing on the opposite side to house a family room.

At right, In the octagonal center hall the stair winds three levels up to a cupola. In the stairwell hangs the original bronze gasolier.

1183 Georgia Avenue
1848
Oliver

In antebellum times professional architects were a scarce commodity and designs for houses were often taken from plan books. And so it was that in 1848 Macon banker Cadwell W. Raines chose a unique design from Rantlett's 1847 plan book, *The Architect*, for a house he built at a prominent site on College Hill. The details of the house were Greek Revival but, instead of the typical floor plan of four rooms over four rooms intersected by central halls, this plan was an innovation. The four principal rooms on each of the three floors formed a cross with porches connecting its arms. This arrangement provided three exposures for each room allowing for maximum ventilation. Additionally, the crux of the cross was an octagonal hall rising to a cupola atop the house. The hall acted as a huge chimney with windows in the cupola allowing the rising hot air to escape. These features made the house ideally suited for a warm climate so it is natural that the only other houses of similar design in the United States are also in the South, one in Advance, North Carolina and another in Columbus, Mississippi.

Situated on the hillside to face Wesleyan College, which stood diagonally across the intersection of Georgia Avenue and College Street, the impressive and unusual house at once became a landmark. In 1978 it was officially designated one by the Department of the Interior, becoming Macon's second National Register Landmark House, the other being the Johnston-Felton-Hay House.

In 1940 the house was deteriorating, serving as a boarding house and being threatened with demolition by an oil company wanting to build a service station on the busy corner. Determined to save the house, a neighbor on College Street, Mr. Alfred Ross Willingham, acquired the property. Two years later he conveyed it to his daughter and son-in-law, Katherine and Joseph Carmichael. The couple renovated the house, carefully preserving its original features including the immense bronze and brass gaslight chandelier in the octagonal hall and even the 1848 vintage paint on decorative trim in the formal rooms. The house again became a family home. In 1951 the house was the setting for the wedding of the Carmichaels' daughter Katherine, affectionately called Kitty, to Lee P. Oliver, Jr. After a tour in the Air Force the couple returned in 1957 to live in the family home.

For many years family and friends gathered in the octagonal hall on Christmas Eve around a tree rising well into the second floor. They sang carols with some guests lining the winding stair. It was a memorable sight. Today a fourth generation enjoys visiting their family home. They use and learn the history of the heirlooms that fill the rooms as well as the story of the grand old house they know as home.

Kitty and Lee Oliver have contributed far more to Macon's architectural heritage than preservation of their own landmark house. Lee is a gifted architect responsible for numerous well-designed local houses. For two decades Kitty both preached and practiced historic preservation as the dedicated Executive Director of the Middle Georgia Historical Society. Fortunately for Macon the preservation genes seem intact in the upcoming generations of Olivers.

At right, The Olivers enjoy sitting on their front porch with its views of historic College Street and Georgia Avenue.

Above, An Oliver family heirloom, a half-tester bed by New Orleans furniture maker Prudent Mallard is quite at home in an upstairs bedroom.

At left, The parlor, furnished with family treasures, is expanded with a bay window which is framed by an ionic portico topped with molding of an unusual wave motif.

Almost unique in its design this cruciform Greek Revival house has been a Macon landmark since 1848.

At right, "welcoming arms" steps lead from the main level of the house to the garden.

607 College Street
1854
Holliday

This overscale, raised cottage sitting high above a full garden level has faced College Street since 1854. It isn't known who designed the house for its original owner, Henry North, but its style is reminiscent of houses in the Mississippi Delta. Its full-width veranda, its basic dimensions, and room arrangement date from that year, as do many of its elegant interior details. But the look of the house was changed dramatically in 1911 by a young architect, Neel Reid. Reid opened the large front dormer in the roof and topped it with a decorative balustrade. He made the veranda more accessible by adding French doors and, most notably, for people passing by, he designed the graceful picket fence and gate at the sidewalk.

From the mid-to-late nineteenth century the W. K. de Graffenreid family occupied the house. A daughter, Claire, was a teacher, world traveler, and nationally published author. In 1886 Theodosius Davies Tinsley, a Confederate veteran, wholesale grocer, and longtime member of the Board of Education purchased the house. He and his family lived here for almost fifty years. The street beside the house bears their name. The Tinsleys' younger daughter, Sarah, was a childhood companion and later dancing partner of Neel Reid who grew up around the corner on Forsyth Street. It was only natural that Mr. Tinsley engaged his daughter's talented young friend to improve the family home. After her marriage Sarah lived the rest of her life in a Reid-designed house just across College Street.

During the Tinsleys' tenure, a young student at Wesleyan (and granddaughter of the College's first President) would often stroll by the house, sometimes pausing to lean on the picket fence and dream of someday living in the beautiful house. And, of course, she did. Her name was Pauline Pierce, or Polly, who married Dr. Ernest Corn. In the 1930s the Corns bought the house and brought up their four children there. Polly, an expert gardener, made it her task to transform the rear garden. She did not change the iron gate and portion of fence salvaged from the site across College Street, previously occupied by the Georgia Academy for the Blind. Polly's gardening expertise was shared with readers of her column on gardening in the *Macon Telegraph*. Her columns were compiled into a book, *Garden Ventures*.

After some fifty years' residence Polly gave up her dream home to another young couple, he also a physician, Peter and Jeanne Holliday. During their extensive renovations to the house, they have installed an up-to-date kitchen and bathrooms while being careful to respect the character of the house. The house is furnished throughout with period antiques including an important collection of Audubon bird prints. Polly's garden has been restored and enhanced and now includes a pool and pool house. As a talented writer Jeanne Holliday upholds the female literary tradition of the house set by Claire de Graffenreid and Polly Corn. Admirers of their house hope that the Hollidays will uphold the residency tradition of the two prior families and make this their home for decades to come.

Above, The front door surround is of beveled leaded glass.

At left, This 1854 Mississippi-style raised cottage was renovated by architect Neel Reid in 1911.

*The library is hung with part of the Holliday
collection of Audubon bird prints.*

Above, A guest bedroom opening on to the stair hall is furnished with period pieces and, over the mantle, a portrait of Jeanne Holliday.

At left, A medieval tapestry hangs in the double parlors where Sidney Lanier once played his flute in a musicale.

The most dramatic change made to the house by
the Hollidays was updating the kitchen while
keeping it true to the character of the house.

Upper left, A view from the garden level under the rear porch and steps makes an interesting contrast in light and shade.

Below left, A scuppernong arbor makes a cool restful spot adjacent to the house.

*Pleasing proportions and delicate
details produce a charming look for this
antebellum cottage.*

920 High Street
1857
Reichert

The ancient Greeks had mathematical formulas to govern the proportions of buildings in order that they achieve perfect aesthetic harmony. The designer of this house must have been acquainted with such formulas. Near perfect proportions, precise symmetry, and delicate ornamentation render this 1857 Victorian cottage a visual magnet. A lyrical cast iron fence separates the flower-filled front yard from the herringbone patterned brick sidewalk and brick-paved High Street. The total composition is authentically nineteenth century.

Nathan Campbell Munroe, planter and businessman, built this house with a typical Macon cottage plan of five rooms with a center hall. Munroe's main residence was "Sylvan Lodge," a Greek Revival house in the nearby village of Vineville. That house is now owned by the Pilot Club, a Macon-based organization for businesswomen. From that house Munroe wrote letters to family members during the War Between the States, which documented life in Macon during that traumatic period. Mr. Munroe's daughter Blanche, married Captain John McIntosh Kell, first mate on the Confederate battleship, the Alabama.

Following the war, the High Street house was bought by Confederate veteran Captain Sam Dunlap. His family farm included the Indian Mounds of the present-day Ocmulgee National Monument. The family house, which still stands, was used as his headquarters by Union General Stoneman during his July, 1864 raid of Macon. Captain Dunlap gave up farming to enter the hardware business in Macon and managed to become quite prosperous during the difficult time of Reconstruction. His growing wealth enabled him to exchange the modest cottage for an impressive white-columned house on College Street. At his death in 1901 Captain Dunlap was interred in a handsome granite mausoleum just inside the main gate at Rose Hill Cemetery.

In the twentieth century the cottage was home to the William A. Snows of an old and distinguished Macon family. Its current owners are Bebe and Albert Reichert, Jr. whose two families go back many generations in Middle Georgia. They have furnished their house with old family pieces as well as simple, honest furnishings they have acquired together. Their rooms are arranged attractively for comfort and convenience and seem to shy away from any notion of pretense. In fact, they are what an admirer pausing in front of this charming and picturesque house would expect to find if fortunate enough to be invited inside.

Upper right, Restraint is apparent in the dining room with the use of plants and old family pieces.

Below right, Antiques appropriate to the age of the house and pleasing soft colors help make a bedroom inviting.

A fireplace in the kitchen is a warming touch in more than one way.

Above, When the house was little more than twenty years old, it was altered to its present appearance. Georgia marble sheathes the porch pillars.

At left, The original Willingham house was "High Victorian" in design.

When this house was built in 1886, it was what was called "High Victorian," adorned with lavish trim, shallow porches, a turret, and a cupola. Its owner was Calder B. Willingham whose family had moved to Macon from South Carolina following the War Between the States. He and his seven brothers became involved in almost every major local business from banking, building, and insurance to cotton manufacturing and real estate. They also made time to be part of almost every worthwhile civic and charitable enterprise.

After Mr. Willingham's death in 1908, his son Alfred Ross Willingham took possession of the house. He was married to the former Kate Coleman, a descendant of some of Macon's earliest settlers. The young couple undertook a complete renovation of the house, eliminating many of the Victorian flourishes. The cupola was removed and a wrap-around porch with marble pillars was added. The effect of the changes was a far more restrained appearance for the house. One Victorian touch, a colorful stained glass window, was left to enliven the stair landing. Also remaining were the original dimensions of the spacious, high-ceilinged rooms, which, opening into each other, create an airy and open arrangement.

The younger Mr. Willingham adhered to the family tradition and pursued many interests in business and civic affairs. He held offices in the family business, Willingham Sash and Door, which continues today. In 1958 a high school was named for him to honor his decades of service on the Board of Public Education. It was he who acted to save the landmark house at 1183 Georgia Avenue from demolition in 1940. He passed it on to his family whose descendants still live there.

In 1972 when Peter and Maryel Battin were moving to Macon, they resisted realty agents' efforts to show them suburban houses. Instead, they responded to the charm of the house created by the Willinghams, father and son. Shortly after moving in and making a home for themselves and two small children, they became involved in their new neighborhood's fledgling preservation movement. In 1975 Peter served as president of the new Macon Heritage Foundation. Several years later Maryel was serving in the same position when she suddenly found herself without an Executive Director to run the organization. The Board of Trustees implored her to take the job. She agreed, and remained for eighteen years, leading the Foundation to success after success. In so doing she became a nationally recognized figure in historic preservation.

Maryel is a proud native of Scotland and the lovely things she has inherited and collected give a decidedly Scottish feel to the rooms of her home. A highlight is a large double portrait by Comer Jennings of daughter, Maia, and son, Ramsay, who is wearing a kilt of the Clan Ramsay tartan. In the dining room a touch of Americana is the Battins' collection of early Steuben glass. Overall this house seems an entirely fitting dwelling for lovers of fine architecture and champions of historic preservation.

*Above, The large, open, and handsome
stair hall lies at the heart of the house.
It is enriched with a fine tall case clock
and an original stained glass window.*

*At right, On the piano in the music
room stands the Steuben vase presented
to Mayrel Battin at the time of her
retirement as long-term director of the
Macon Heritage Foundation.*

Above, Traces of Maryel Battin's Scottish background can be detected in the living room.

At left, An open floor plan affords a vista from the dining room through the living room into the music room. Part of Mrs. Battin's collection of vintage Steuben glass is in lighted cases.

1085 Georgia Avenue
1887
Cerny

Irish immigrant Christopher Burke came to Macon in the 1850s to do faux finish painting for William B. Johnston at his newly-built Italian villa. He liked the town and decided to settle and open a paint store. In time he and his son, Thomas, expanded the store into a hardware and building supplies business. They prospered so well, that in 1887 Thomas built for himself this gem of a Queen Anne Victorian house. It is only a short distance up the hill from Mr. Johnston's villa, now known as the Hay House.

The architect's lively medley of stained glass, turret, bay, gables, and porches keeps the eye engaged as it takes in all the elements of the façade. The rounded section of the front porch was added by Neel Reid in an early twentieth-century renovation. Also at that time the house was almost doubled in size with a rear addition, and the interior was relieved of much of its Victorian ornamentation and outfitted with Georgian details. Reid was a contemporary and friend of Thomas Burke's daughters, Miss May and Miss Martina Burke. On his travels he selected English and European antiques for them to use in redecorating the house. The sisters lived in the house until their deaths in the 1960s. Having no direct heirs they bequeathed their family fortune to a philanthropic trust, the T. C. Burke Foundation, which provides assistance to terminally ill cancer patients.

In the years following the Burke ownership, the house was used as a stylish antique shop and, later, as a drug rehabilitation facility. In the late 1970s the house was bought and renovated by Dr. and Mrs. L. E. Brown who brought up their three children here. The Browns were among a new wave of preservation pioneers whose revitalization efforts breathed new life and vitality into what was a deteriorating neighborhood.

At the beginning of the twenty-first century another young couple acquired the house and are bringing up their three children here. Andy and Lyn Cerny use their entire large house as a comfortable family home. They have furnished it with a pleasing blend of antiques and contemporary pieces, but are careful to preserve period details such as the original plumbing fixtures. Among the unique features of this house are a stained glass window in the center of a chimney and the largest butler's pantry in Macon. A trap door in the attic gives access to a flat roof, which offers a panoramic view of downtown Macon. Immediately behind the house is a delightful carriage house cleverly adapted for use as two apartments. If the Burkes could return and find their house filled with toys, kittens, and fun they would have to be pleased.

Neel Reid added the rounded porch to the classic Queen Anne façade of the Burke House.

Above, The Burkes had the finest of hardware in their bathrooms.

At right, Claw-foot bathtubs are popular today and this may be the ultimate example.

The very large room used for dining by
the Burke family has been adapted as a
family room by the Cernys.

Above, Victorian features of the parlor include stained glass and a round turret.

At right, Neel Reid classicized interior details of the house for his friends, the Burke sisters. This library attests to his success.

An arched stained glass window inset into a chimney enlivens a children's playroom.

In 1950, when it was a half century old, this house was transformed from a simple farm house into an English Regency style house. The vintage architectural firm of Dennis and Dennis planned the transformation.

3395 Osborne Place
1900
Faircloth

At the turn of the twentieth century this house started its life as a simple farm house in the middle of agricultural land miles from the limits of the town of Macon. It was after World War I that rapidly increasing ownership of automobiles made possible the extension of Macon into new suburbs. Among the new developments was Ingleside, a large, hilly, and heavily wooded section, which incorporated the grounds of a recently closed amusement park. Crump's Park had been, literally, the end of the line—the farthest point the street cars traveled from downtown Macon. It was a frequent destination for Maconites who enjoyed its casino, theater, dance pavilion, and swimming facilities. Among the streets of the popular new neighborhood was Osborne Place, which was cut just in front of this farm house. It was a short street but one soon lined with charming houses.

When it was half a century old the farm house was transformed by its owners, Mr. and Mrs. Leo Huckabee, Sr. Under the direction of Marjorie Huckabee's talented cousin, Charles Townsend of W. E. Browne Decorating Company in Atlanta, and architectural consultant, David Richmond Byers, III, the old four-square structure was taken back in time to the era of the English Regency. The house acquired a graceful portico with Ionic columns and welcoming arms steps. It also grew wings, additions to each side with new arched windows affording space for a formal drawing room to one side, and a generous sun porch on the other. Interior walls were removed to allow a new combination entry and stair hall to extend the entire width of the original house. The exterior wall of the dining room was breeched to install a bow window, which opened that room to the out doors. Sophisticated moldings, innovative folding doors, and a cove ceiling gave cachet to the formal rooms. Having completed the setting, Mr. Townsend began a search for the proper furnishings. Among the treasures he found were an eighteenth-century tester bed and, in London, a magnificent Georgian breakfront.

Almost twenty-five years ago Mr. and Mrs. Tee Faircloth chose this handsome house in which to raise their two young children. Aside from updating the kitchen and bathrooms, the Faircloths have kept the essence of the house much as Mrs. Huckabee and her advisors left it. Among the treasures Gay has found and placed perfectly are the tester bed and the impressive breakfront Mr. Townsend had found for the Huckabees, which are now returned to their rightful places. Another dramatic find is the pair of neoclassical consoles, designed by noted Atlanta architect Philip Trammell Shutze, which look very much as if he had planned their use in the Faircloths' entry hall.

The simple farm house, which was built more than a century ago, was subsequently transformed into a classic. And classics, by definition, have no need of change.

Above, Architectural remnants from early houses were salvaged and used to lend authenticity to this house.

At right, A tester bed chosen for the house by noted decorator Charles Townsend is the centerpiece of the guest bedroom.

*In the west wing added to the house is the
drawing room with its high-coved ceiling.*

*A bow window in the dining room wall
provides light into the room and a view
of the gardens beyond.*

Interesting architectural design and attention to detail are continued in the family's breakfast room.

*A wing added to the eastern side of the
house encompasses a generous sun porch.*

*Walls between the front rooms of the
original farm house were removed to
create an entry and stair hall that extends
the width of the original house.*

Above, Neel Reid was playful with the square windows with starburst muntins and lattice work to support climbing vines.

Neel Reid often adapted traditional designs to include large porches and provided access to them with French doors. The pale green color for shutters was specified by Mr. Reid.

1962 Forsyth Street
1908
Barfield

The children of the present owner of this property are the sixth generation to live here. They live in the oldest surviving house designed by Neel Reid who was a friend of, and architect for, their grandmother's grandmother. In 1908 Reid returned to Macon after completing his architectural education with a tour of Europe. Mrs. Helen Gustin Logan asked Reid, who was just beginning an architectural practice, to design a house for her two daughters, Louise Logan Clisby and Georgia Logan Redding, on property the Gustin family had owned since antebellum times. The result is the vernacular Georgian house pictured here.

Most of Reid's earliest houses were variations on a Colonial Revival theme. And, throughout his career, he repeated certain elements that came to be identified with his work. This house is a precursor of those design choices, which would propel the recent graduate into a career as Georgia's most celebrated architect. Reid began this house with the standard arrangement for a Georgian house. He added to it the features, which would become trademarks of his work, including French doors, window boxes, and a low terrace spanning the width of the house. Inside, his plan also altered the typical floor plan with unique Reid ideas. Reid's halls were almost always oversized to give a feeling of spaciousness even in small houses. His houses always were oriented to the outside with large areas of glass and lots of windows and doors. Reid also insisted on fireplaces in almost every room even in his houses which were equipped with central furnaces. All of these elements typical of the architect are evident in this early house.

Louise Logan Barfield now owns her grandmother's house. She is a concert pianist and owner and director of the Little Carnegie of the South, a concert hall and art gallery for emerging and established performing and visual artists. This intimate center for the arts is located in the house next door to Louise's home on property owned by her great, great grandparents. In her home she literally cannot turn around without touching something that belonged to her Gustin, Logan, Clisby, or Barfield antecedents. Furniture, portraits, and a host of pianos keep Louise and her children, Logan and Clisby, in touch with their family history as well as their musical heritage.

Louise Barfield's living room may be unique in Macon in that it houses three grand pianos. Ms. Barfield is pictured at her mid-nineteenth century Steinway in the portrait above the fireplace by Catharine Burns Liles.

Family heirlooms grace the entry-stair hall. Windows at the stair landing once opened onto a screened porch now enclosed for use as a sitting room.

Leaded glass of the double front doors and fanlight above signals hospitality to visitors.

340 College Street
1908
Whitten

Shortly after the turn of the twentieth century Americans were swept by a passion for architecture refined from styles that had predominated in the early republic. While in other parts of the country people chose Georgian or Federal models, in the South, and decidedly in Macon, the taste was for the Greek Revival. This choice sprang from a nostalgia for the Old South and its architectural traditions. Many of the white-columned façades of College Street, in fact, date from this period a century ago rather than from antebellum times. This house is a splendid example of the Classic Revival movement. It was the favorite Macon house of playwright Tennessee Williams who lived in the neighborhood in the early 1940s and whose dramas often had themes of Southerners' nostalgia for a vanished past.

The cast iron fence at the sidewalk is an example of authenticity in a historic landscape. The early photographs of College Street reveal that uniformly its houses had similar fences to separate them from the street. The highest order of Greek columns, Corinthian, was used in the colonnade which bows outward to welcome the approaching guest. All the elements of the façade are symmetrical including the handsome double entrance doors inset with leaded and beveled glass. Inside, the large, high-ceilinged rooms feature wide openings between them providing a feeling of openness and affording the opportunity for entertaining on a grand scale.

The house was constructed in 1908 for the George Turpin family. Their daughter, Cecil Antoinette, was said by her contemporaries to be "the prettiest girl in Macon." Later, the Walter J. Grace, Jr. family called this house home and, later still, the J. Freeman Hart, Jr. family lived here. The Harts, known to their many friends as Buster and Bessie, annually opened their house for a large Christmas party which was a highlight of the holiday season. In 1964 the Middle Georgia Historical Society was organized at a meeting hosted here by the Harts.

Continuing the tradition of hospitality, the current owners of the house, Rick and Sue Whitten, make good use of their home by entertaining friends. And, recognizing that they are stewards of a historic asset, they frequently allow charitable organizations to host parties here. The Whittens, who undertook an ambitious renovation of the house, were helped by C. Terry Holland, ASID, in outfitting the house for the twenty-first century. Vibrant colors, and an eclectic collection of art, complement the mellow antiques used to furnish the rooms and provide an appropriate and inviting setting for family life and lively parties.

*Double front doors open into a room which
serves as a foyer, parlor, and stairhall.*

A handsome fireplace is the focal point in
the front parlor.

A comfortable family sitting room at the rear of the house looks out into a walled courtyard with carriage house beyond.

An elaborate plaster ceiling medallion is accented with color in the dining room.

The two important early nineteenth-century Greek Revival houses that face Jefferson Terrace originally had lawns that descended all the way to Georgia Avenue. In the first decade of the twentieth century a new street was cut through the middle of these lawns. It was named for Thomas Jefferson, following a precedent in the neighborhood of naming streets for early presidents. Three separate property owners on this short new street engaged the rising young architect, Neel Reid, to design houses for their small new lots. At this time, early in his career, Reid had become infatuated with medieval English architecture and was using it often in his Macon commissions. He enjoyed applying Arts and Crafts details from his own time to Tudor, Gothic, and Elizabethan precedents. How well he succeeded can be seen on Jefferson Terrace. The first part of the western side of the street seems almost like a lane in an old English village with the mullioned windows in the half-timbered façades of the houses built right on the street.

Neel Reid's greatest challenge and most successful solution was in the house he designed, in 1910, for Mr. Walter T. Johnson. Cutting the new street created a narrow triangular lot at the College Street end. Reid's challenge was to fulfill his client's requirements for a spacious house with gracious rooms set on a small triangle. His solution was to create a series of planes, the house expanding in depth as the lot size increased. The result is a triumph. The narrowest part of the lot has room for a brick porch topped with crenellation and opened by arches overlooking the diminutive garden at the point of the triangle. The main body of the house of three floors steps out, then steps out again toward Georgia Avenue as the lot expands. A series of gable ends, alternately brick and half-timbered, encircle the roof line. Beside the entry a mammoth chimney of intricate brickwork rises the full height of the house and is decorated with a terra cotta swastika that conceals a bolt for securing the chimney to the roof. The roof of the entry stoop repeats the angles of the gables and is supported by a fretwork of timber. A pair of built-in benches face each other creating an alfresco inglenook. The stair hall windows are stepped to follow the staircase and the proportions of window-to-wall are reminiscent of the Elizabethan Hardwick Hall, "more glass than wall."

Maybe because it is a town house with almost no yard to maintain, the house was an attractive target for Macon's pioneer preservationists. Early in the 1970s Neede Goode and Clyde Windham bought it and erased the traces of its lengthy use as a real estate office. Dr. and Mrs. Joseph Shields became its next custodians and cared for it for two decades. When Joe retired to his native Mississippi, Katherine Kennedy Walden bought the house and undertook its most recent renovation. She is an interior designer and a Macon native who loves fine architecture, having lived in a number of historic houses. With her two sons grown, Katherine found the Neel Reid townhouse a perfect home for her, providing enough extra room for her office and design studio. She can park literally at her front door, a real convenience when toting files or fabric samples. Katherine's treatment of her own interior reveals her love of color, her willingness to do the unexpected, and her ability to mix the old with the new. Neel Reid would be pleased.

Medieval English is the look intended for this house by its architect, Neel Reid.

Built-in bookshelves are one of Neel Reid's
space-saving features for the living room.

Above, Neel Reid was a master of detail as he demonstrated with this stair hall.

At left, Not quite an inglenook, but close, is this fireplace vestibule adjoining the living room.

Above, Casement windows in the dining room look onto an urban streetscape.

At right, Katharine Walden has outfitted the upstairs hall as a living space. Original blueprints for the house hang above a drop-leaf table.

Designer Katharine Walden has made use of
a sunporch to house her studio and office.

For more than eighty years a Macon landmark,
this red brick Georgian house was designed by
Elliott Dunwody, Jr.

Since 1922 this landmark has stood with regal aplomb on its prominent corner. Generations of people passing by have paused to admire its impressive façade. They might well wonder how its architect managed to make it seem grand while, at the same time, welcoming. The young architect who achieved this feat was W. Elliott Dunwody, Jr.. Mr. Dunwody began his career in 1914 after completing his studies at the Georgia Institute of Technology. He contributed well-designed and significant buildings to the local landscape and beyond for much of the twentieth century. The firm he headed continues under the direction of the second and third generations of his family. Mr. Dunwody was a classicist drawing his ideas from the great buildings of the past and adapting them to modern requirements. In that tradition he designed most of the original buildings at the Wesleyan College Campus at Rivoli as well as buildings at Mercer University.

Many years after it happened, Elliott Dunwody's widow related the story of their first date. She was Mary Bennett Cox and Elliott (he never liked being addressed as Mr. Dunwody) called for her in his automobile at her home near downtown Macon. Driving slowly out Vineville Avenue Elliott asked her opinion of many of the houses they passed. When they reached the intersection of Pierce and Pio Nono Avenues he pointed to the handsome Georgian house on the corner and said, "And what do you think of that one?" She replied, "Why, it's the most beautiful house in Macon." His expression told her that she had passed his test, and she always believed that her answer had cemented their relationship.

A number of houses designed by Elliott Dunwody are still occupied by the families for whom they were built and this is one of them. Mr. and Mrs. John D. Comer commissioned him to design a house for them. Mr. Comer was an executive with the Bibb Manufacturing Company. When he tragically died of pneumonia while the house was under construction, Mrs. Comer instructed Mr. Dunwody to complete the house for her and their children.

The house was decorated originally by the firm of Lindsay and Morgan of Savannah. In 1935, Mrs. Comer consulted Charles Townsend of W. E. Browne Decorating Company in Atlanta, to oversee decoration of her drawing room. Among the important pieces he found and installed were an elaborate Chinese Chippendale mirror hung above the mantle and an eighteenth-century English breakfront.

In 1962, after Mrs. Comer's death, her son, John, and his wife, Mary Anderson Comer, came to live in the house. Mary had grown up in an Elliott Dunwody designed house only a block away. Although they introduced much of their own furniture into the house, very little of the original decoration was altered. Photographs taken by the Dunwody firm when the house was new show furniture arrangements unchanged in seventy years.

Inside and out, the classic house has a decidedly eighteenth-century Georgian feel. Its mass, its dormers, and its lovely doorway with lacy fanlight reinforce this. But it is not a slavish copy. Among the departures from form are the French windows, wide front terrace, and Palladian arched porch on the east side.

The current John Comer, a prominent Macon attorney, enjoys yard work and is amused when people passing by see him hard at work in serviceable clothes and mistake him for the yard man. One special chore shared with the family each Christmas is hanging colored lights on the enormous cedar tree in the front yard. It's not only a family tradition, it's a Macon tradition. And so is the habit, when struggling through traffic at this busy corner, of glancing over at the serene and handsome house in its frame of leafy green and being rewarded with a moment of calm.

The dining room is faithful to eighteenth-century design with its elaborate molding, wood-paneled walls, and arched cabinets.

A highlight of the Comer House is the elaborate stair with its lyrical proportions.

The living room is furnished with family pieces including some whimsical touches. It opens into a family sitting room.

*Beautiful furnishings placed in the drawing
room in 1935 remain in place today.*

Above, When the house was new in 1923 landscaping was minimal.

At right, This classic revival house of cream brick construction is now buffered from Vineville Avenue traffic by a stand of large old trees.

3557 Vineville Avenue

1923

Rader

Vineville Avenue was not a busy thoroughfare when this house was constructed on it in 1923. In the years immediately following World War I the new streets of the Ingleside subdivision had been cut through farm land. This far out the avenue was still considered the Forsyth Road and was beyond the official limits of Macon. The Classic Revival house, constructed of fashionable cream-colored brick, had a definitely rural aspect. It was built for the family of Wit Jackson, who owned the Union Dry Goods Company. It is said that each of those thousands of fashionable bricks used in its walls cost one dollar.

The house featured large rooms, beautifully detailed and arranged for easy flow around a central stair hall. In the days before air conditioning porches were used as outdoor living rooms and here the architect provided generous porches accessible from the formal rooms. The graceful stair rises to the second level of ample bedrooms, including a master suite, an idea used often in houses built today, but rarely so in the early 1920s. On a corner lot, the house was sited close to the streets rather than centering it on the property. This siting allowed larger side and rear gardens. An early photograph shows the house sitting on a barren lot without trees or shrubbery. Today the gardens are planted beautifully with mature trees and shrubs. Rows of boxwood create formal garden rooms peopled with antique statuary.

Just after the end of World War II a young couple, Mr. and Mrs. C. Richard Rader, purchased the house. Dick Rader was a jeweler. He acquired the old and distinguished firm of S. L. Orr Co., gave it his name and led it to become Macon's premiere jewelry store. Now his son, C. Richard Rader, Jr., continues the traditions set by his father, including an emphasis on antique and estate jewelry.

The Raders' appreciation of the quality and workmanship inherent in old things helps account for the collection of fine antiques used to furnish their home. Especially noteworthy are the antique Oriental rugs that cover the floors, a collection as fine as any in Macon. Above the stately mantle in the living room is a full-length portrait of Margaret, Mrs. Rader, by local artist Hope Hayes. For many years Mrs. Hayes was Macon's most talented and successful portrait artist and her portrait of Margaret Rader captures her beauty as well as her warm personality. Nearby, in his paneled study, hangs a portrait of the late Dick Rader and in an ashtray beneath it rests his ever-present pipe. The faces in the portraits seem to survey with quiet pride the home they shared with each other and their children.

*Iron balusters give
a light feel to the
staircase located in
the rear center of
the house.*

*A portrait of Margaret Rader by local artist
Hope Hayes overlooks the elegantly furnished
living room.*

The presence of the late Dick Rader is still strong in his panelled study with his portrait above the mantle and his pipe resting in a dish on a low table below.

*A tester bed is the nucleus of
the suite of rooms occupying the
western portion of the house's
upper level.*

1158 Oakcliff Road
1927
Chapman

Transferred from the shores of the Mediterranean to the banks of a creek in Macon's Shirley Hills, this villa reflects an architectural style that had grown popular in the United States at the time this house was built in 1927. Although more common in the southern part of California and Florida than in Macon, Mediterranean villas are a logical response to the Middle Georgia climate. This example was one of the early houses built in Shirley Hills, a post World War I development of land owned by the late U.S. Senator A. O. Bacon. Shirley was the name of the Senator's granddaughter. The Frederick Law Olmstead landscaping firm of New York made plans for the subdivision taking advantage of the dramatic hills, slopes, and valleys that were part of the terrain and attempting to preserve its old growth trees. Shirley Hills is now a National Register Historic District.

The family responsible for this house, the Herbert Maro Blocks, also deserve credit for a number of other significant houses in Macon including a 1903 Italianate palazzo built by his parents on College Street. Mr. Block was a leading Macon businessman and operator of the Hotel Dempsey, for decades the town's leading hostelry.

The house was designed by a New Jersey architect who never saw the finished project. It is sheathed in unfinished stucco, floored with hardwood, quarry and glazed tile, and topped with a copper dome above its circular stair. Typically, levels often change between rooms. Wrought iron is a decorative motif inside and out. A large side porch adjoins the living room and offers panoramic views of the gardens. All of these elements are true to the house's Mediterranean origins.

The extensive grounds surrounding the house have been enhanced by its various owners. Among the trees Mr. Block built a log cabin, which was enjoyed by his two young sons. The next owner, C. W. Farmer, dammed the stream below the house to create a small lake and built an authentic looking mill house of river rock complete with a mill wheel. The E. Raymond Smiths lived here next, adding the pool and enlarging the breakfast room.

At the turn of the twenty-first century, Dr. and Mrs. James Chapman and their three children make their home here. They and their designer, Bonnie Starr, have respected the integrity of the romantic architecture. Sparingly using American and Continental pieces of high quality, and interspersing rare pieces of African art from a collection they inherited, they have created a look that fits seamlessly in their Mediterranean villa.

The New Jersey architect never saw this Mediterranean villa he designed for Macon's Shirley Hills neighborhood.

*The swimming pool is one of several
additions to the original house and garden.*

*The house's second owner built this authentic
mill house of native river rock.*

Mexican tiles provide a colorful background for a family sitting room.

*An enclosed porch offers a panoramic view of
the grounds and an ideal spot for a pianist.*

In decorating their house the Chapman family has respected the integrity of the architecture as here in the living room. The portrait above the fireplace is of Jim Chapman's great great grandfather, Isaac Hardeman, a Macon pioneer.

*The stair hall
is authentically
Mediterranean with its
iron railing and arched
niche. Atop it is a copper-
covered dome.*

This amazing house inspires superlatives. The most interesting, the most unusual, the most exuberant, and, certainly, the most Italian are a few it has inspired. It is unquestionably a masterpiece of architecture, but whose exactly has been questioned. Calder W. Payne, who was Macon's leading architectural historian, said that Mrs. Horgan, for whom the house was built, told him that the plans for the house were on Neel Reid's drawing board when he died. Others attribute the house to Philip Trammell Shutze who worked in Neel Reid's firm. Although the exact truth may never be known, it seems certain that Reid was involved in the planning of the house and that Shutze oversaw its construction after Reid's death. Both men had traveled in Italy and either could have found the inspiration for this house in its prototype, the chapel of the Villa Arvedi just north of Verona.

Neel Reid's death in 1926, at the age of forty-one, was a tragedy on several levels. A victim of brain tumors, he was carried on a stretcher on the day before he died to supervise work on a current project. His Atlanta friends chartered a train to Macon to attend his funeral. He is buried in Rose Hill Cemetery. His legacy has been upheld by large numbers of admirers who have made shrines of the buildings he designed. As with many of his clients, Mr. and Mrs. Horgan had been friends of Reid's before seeking his services as architect. The Horgans owned the Idle Hour Nurseries and chose a site for their house on the edge of the property facing the new campus of Wesleyan College.

The Horgans' house is a Baroque composition of fanciful elements accented in convivial colors, as harmonious and as playful as a capriccio. The authentic Italian feeling persists on the interior in which a cruciform hall is centered by a sky-lit dome. Flourishes in trim and molding as well as vaults and groins, marble, plasterwork and old wood all whisper of Italy. And after eighty years all the finishes have the mellow patina of time.

It was in 1965 that Elizabeth Hay McCook purchased the house. The changes she made were technical, not aesthetic. Local architect Delmar Warren designed a setting for the house, Italian gardens enclosed with a colorful stucco wall and wooden gates. When Mrs. McCook called Atlanta decorator Charles Townsend to tell him she had bought the Horgan house he replied, "Your wallpaper was ordered yesterday!" After seeing it, she agreed, and it still seems right for the room. Betty McCook's greatest addition to the house was a pair of seventeenth-century embroidered panels commissioned by the Principessa Albicini of Forli, Italy. An invalid, the noblewoman devoted the last years of her life to the production of the embroideries. She imported thirty French seamstresses who worked for sixteen years to complete them. The exquisite panels are hung flanking the dining room mantle and, in honor of the panels and the Principessa, the house was named the Villa Albicini.

Other furnishings throughout the house continue the Italian theme. Many, especially silver and porcelain, are from the home of Betty Hay's parents, the P. L. Hays of the Georgia Trust for Historic Preservation's Hay House.

Although exquisitely detailed and sumptuously furnished, the house is neither large nor grand. It is human in scale. In 1970, Betty McCook married Colonel Joseph R. Curtis and since then they have used the house as their comfortable home. But, in Macon, and in any other place, very few houses can match the Villa Albicini for living in style.

Based on the design of the chapel of an Italian villa this house was one of architect Neel Reid's last projects before his death at the age of 41.

Authentically Italian, the marble floored entry hall opens into an octagonal center hall lit by a skylight in its dome.

*Simulating an open loggia this glass enclosed room
is used by the family as their sitting room.*

The family often takes meals in the beautifully detailed breakfast room.

Graceful curves are worked into the plaster of the living room ceiling.

*In the dining room the Albicini panels, which
gave the house its name, flank the fireplace.*

French embroiderers at the Palazzo Albicini in Forli, Italy created these panels in the seventeenth century.

*While the entrance to this 1927 Georgian cottage faces
Cleveland Avenue, architect Elliott Dunwody provided an
equally handsome elevation to face busy Vineville Avenue.*

114 Cleveland Avenue
1928
Hogan

This compact Georgian Revival cottage provides its occupants a good deal more space than its outward appearance suggests. It was designed in 1928 by W. Elliott Dunwody, Jr., a young architect then entering the prime of his long career. His client was Mr. W. D. Anderson, president of the Bibb Manufacturing Company, who wanted a house for his daughter and son-in-law, Mr. and Mrs. McKibben Lane. Mr. Anderson chose well. Elliott Dunwody's style of choice was Classic Revival and this house demonstrates his flair for that genre. Although the Lanes were well pleased with their house, within a few years the growth of their family compelled them to build a new house nearby on Hines Terrace. They always remembered fondly their days in the "wee cottage."

In the ensuing years the house had numerous owners, including the family of Mr. C. O. McAfee, candy manufacturer and public-spirited citizen. In 2000 it was bought by Dr. and Mrs. Jasper T. Hogan, Jr. The Hogans were empty-nesters, downsizing from the very large landmark house on College Street they had reno-vated some twenty years earlier. Having been well-acquainted with its architect and its original owners, they felt an immediate affinity for the house, which was reinforced by its good details and generous spaces in a compact arrangement. Entry is through a small vestibule into a large living room. At the far end of the room French doors beside a fireplace give access to a double porch with columns supporting a graceful arch. At the near end of the room is a double width opening to a sizeable dining room. Beyond is an efficiently arranged up-to-date kitchen and eating area. A small central hall in the center of the house leads to a bedroom and a cozy sitting room. Interior stairs rise to two bedrooms under the eaves in the half story above.

Although they wanted to make some changes to the house, the Hogan's real challenge was to condense their sizable collections of art, books, furniture, rugs, silver, and porcelain. Among their treasures are pieces from the estate of the Misses May and Martina Burke, including a magnificent red japanned secretary from Venice, which was purchased in London by Neel Reid.

Jean Hogan and her partner, Mary Sheridan, own Valentino Interiors and have created some of Macon's most appealing interior spaces. Jasper (Jap) Hogan is a Renaissance man who excels in several areas, includ-ing medicine, gourmet cooking, and gardening. He is also something of an authority on antiques, especially early porcelain and silver. Together these two made a formidable team in the editing process. Keeping and in-corporating the best of the best they have made the wee cottage the most elegant house of its size in Macon.

The Hogan's dining room is not only beautifully appointed, it is the scene of some of Macon's best dinners. Dr. Hogan is a gourmet chef.

*Rooms in the cottage are surprisingly large.
In the living room are the Venetian secretary
bought in London by Neel Reid and a
chinoiserie medals cabinet.*

The small house is set on a small lot, but
with adequate room for a charming walled
courtyard.

At the rear of the Hogan house is a small
informal sitting room.

The Thornsberrys were successful in creating a weathered finish on the stucco of their Italian Villa.

2694 Stanislaus Circle
1929
Thornsberry

As the decade called the Roaring Twenties came to a close, Macon saw the creation of its last great house to be completed before the onset of the Great Depression. The house was a fitting climax to a prosperous decade in which a wealth of stylish houses had been added to Macon's architectural treasury. In 1929, Mr. and Mrs. Morris Michael employed Philip Trammell Shutze, principal designer of the firm of Hentz, Adler and Shutze, to design for them a Tuscan house with Spanish touches. Mr. Shutze only recently had filled the place of the deceased Neel Reid in the firm he had joined in 1919. The Michaels no doubt had seen examples of Mr. Shutze's work in Atlanta where he indulged his passion for Italian Baroque. Whether due to the Michael's preference, or his own changing tastes, Mr. Shutze used far more restraint in this design. Though enriched with ornamental details, and hardly plain, this house is devoid of the swags, garlands, and undulant parapets the architect had emphasized in some earlier designs.

Mr. Michael named his new house the Villa Theresa in honor of his wife. The couple employed the noted decorative artist, Athos Menaboni, to do marbleizing and other decorative painting in the house. Mr. Menaboni assisted in fitting an antique French paper mural of Venice in the dining room. The completed house was a series of amazing spaces, from the graveled forecourt through the cross hall with arched niches which leads to the soaring hexagonal stair hall with its circular stair. On the left is a drawing room, which seems plucked from Tuscany. On the right is a library with beamed ceiling, terrazzo floor, and an interior fountain. In every direction the eye discovers a new delight. Outside, the visual treats continue with an arched loggia, a walled courtyard, a reflecting pool, and an outdoor living room.

The Michaels owned the Villa Theresa for a quarter of a century. In 1954, the William P. Simmons family took possession. They brought with them something new to the house, children. Few changes were made, but a swimming pool was added for the children and their friends. Bill Simmons was president of the Southern Crate and Veneer Company, then president of the First National Bank. He was also an accomplished artist and generous patron of the arts. His wife, Betty Sweet, is a much-loved figure in Macon, supporting every good cause and present at every worthwhile event. The Simmons family loved the house for more than forty years.

In 2000, Dr. and Mrs. Robert Thornsberry bought the house and have made extensive, yet sensitive, changes including an expanded kitchen that blends without seeming effort into its surroundings. Their designer, Sally Sinclair Hershner, shares a feeling for Italy with Starling Thornsberry that keeps their ideas authentic. It was a major project to achieve the right gradations of color for the exterior stucco. It succeeded, and the Villa Theresa looks as if the color has aged, weathered, and faded over centuries. The huge magnolias near the street were trimmed so that now even strangers can enjoy what Mr. Shutze and the Michaels achieved, the splendid Villa Theresa.

Above, Alternating squares of grass and paving create a checkerboard effect in the garden by the pool.

At right, A loggia opening to a walled courtyard on the southern wing of the house is an ideal spot for atmospheric dining.

Above, An impish creature serves as sentinel in the garden.

At left, The Thornsberrys created this inviting outdoor living room complete with fireplace.

The library has an appropriately Mediterranean feel with its beamed ceiling, columns and interior fountain.

*French wallpaper with scenes of Venice visually
expands the dining room. Faux finishes original to
the house are by noted artist Athos Menaboni.*

Understated elegance describes the living room. Many of the colorful paintings in the house are by Starling Thornsberry.

Grand and authentic are two correct adjectives for the central stair hall.

The exterior of the house that architect Ellamae Ellis League built for herself in 1941 appears rustic with its unpainted siding and shake roof, but is in fact quite sophisticated.

1790 Waverland Drive
1941
McCleary

This house represents both a radical departure in residential architecture and a tribute to the talent of the remarkable architect who built it to be her home. In 1922 Ellamae Ellis League found herself a single mother with two small children to support. Taking a clerical job in an architect's office, Mrs. League was able to learn about the profession. A lady with gumption, she embarked for Paris to study at the Ecole des Beaux Arts. After her return to Macon she became an apprentice and at last an architect. Even during the depression she secured commissions for houses large and small as well as churches, school, and hospitals. Originally she worked in the Neoclassical style of her mentor, William Oliphant. As time went by she investigated bolder approaches. Her daughter, Jean, was in architectural school at Harvard with disciples of the Bauhaus school of architecture and she influenced her mother's ideas.

After World War II, Mrs. League operated her office as an atelier, a studio where young architects could gain experience while exchanging ideas. Many successful Macon architects got their start in Mrs. League's office and have fond memories of its stimulating atmosphere.

Later in her career Mrs. League received a rare honor when she was made a Fellow of the American Institute of Architects. Such an honor was so unusual for someone of her gender that her citation was inscribed to "Mr." Ellamae Ellis League. Mrs. League never asked them to change it. She had no patience with anyone who tried to credit her with being a "woman" architect. She said, "I am an architect. Period."

By 1940, Mrs. League was ready to design a house for herself. The depression was easing, her children were leaving home, and she had definite ideas for a house built expressly for her. What she created is like no other house. It has no identifiable style. It could be called "rustic" as it is of frame construction, with redwood siding which was allowed to weather to a dark gray-brown, and has a wood shake roof. But the house is far more sophisticated than a first glance might reveal. Large, multi-paned windows allow views from, and light into, the rooms. The house is on four levels. Family entry is from the garage. Steps lead to the main level, which includes a hall, living room, dining room, and kitchen. More steps lead up to a bath and the master bedroom. The highest level is a second bedroom or office, which opens onto a private roof deck. The living room is the largest space in the house and made to seem larger with a mirrored wall on its far end into which a fireplace is set. The room seems open to the out-of-doors via a large window, flanked by two doors, opening to a terrace at the rear of the house. From the terrace, steep steps, almost a ladder, lead to the roof deck above. It was here that Mrs. League staged salons where her friends and office staff congregated on Sundays.

The house was completed at the end of 1941, and Mrs. League lived here half a century until her death. The second owner is Dennis McCleary, Director of Music for Vineville United Methodist Church. Dennis has purposefully made minimal changes to the house and has worked hard to have Mrs. League's accomplishment recognized by having her house listed on the National Register of Historic Places.

The dining room is extended visually with an end wall of three floor-to-ceiling windows. Musician owner Dennis McCleary houses his antique organ in a corner.

The living room seems even larger than it is thanks to a mirrored fireplace wall and picture window with oversized panes.

*Architect Harry A. "Bo" MacEwen designed
this Greek Revival style house for Mr. and Mrs.
William A. Fickling in 1948.*

2929 Ingleside Avenue
1949
Fickling

This Greek Revival style house on the crest of a hill in Ingleside is a mid-twentieth century vision of an antebellum plantation house. The vision belonged to Mr. and Mrs. William A. Fickling, Sr. who had architect Harry A. "Bo" MacEwen make their vision a reality. Bo MacEwen was a principal in the firm of MacEwen, Hall and Ferguson in 1948 when he designed the house for the Ficklings. The street in front of their house, now its driveway, was called Melanie; the street behind, Ashley. Whether the two more sympathetic characters from *Gone With the Wind* had anything to do with the style chosen for the house is unclear. Its floor plan emulates the expected, traditional arrangement of rooms with modifications to accommodate a kitchen adjacent to the dining room.

Mr. Fickling arrived in Macon from his native Butler as a very young man and at once took a job in real estate with Mr. Washington Dessau. Eleven years later he formed his own firm and two years after that he became partners with Mr. B. Sanders Walker in Fickling and Walker, Inc. While building his firm to close the largest number of real estate transactions in Macon, Mr. Fickling found time to devote to numerous activities including his church, Mulberry Methodist, as well as professional, fraternal, civic, and political organizations.

It was later in life that Mr. Fickling made the contribution to his community that would bring him the most recognition, Macon's Cherry Blossom Festival. He found growing in his yard a small shrub with white blossoms tinged with pale pink. Using cuttings he propagated the plants and began giving them to friends. Research revealed to him that his discovery was the Yoshino Cherry tree from Japan. As the trees grew larger their blossoms produced a spectacular effect. Coincidentally the trees usually bloom the week of Mr. Fickling's birthday, the third week in March. Starting from the original tree, more than 200,000 cherry trees now bloom in Macon. The festival he helped begin attracts thousands of visitors from around the world. A large percentage of those visitors drive by the Fickling house on Ingleside to see the hillside covered with blooms. Motor coaches stop to let their passengers walk up the driveway to photograph the trees.

Mr. Fickling's grandson, William A. Fickling, III, and his wife, Shannon, who is an architect, and their children live in the family home. For the duration of the Cherry Blossom Festival they graciously accommodate the hordes of visitors. After all, the children are the fourth generation of Ficklings to occupy the birthplace of the Cherry Blossom Festival.

At right, The spacious stair hall evokes the feeling of an antebellum Greek Revival house.

Above, Wood paneling in the Ficklings' library was milled from trees from the family farm at Rivoli. The wood was atypically almost knot-free.

An English touch at the library fireplace is the hearth bench, a cozy seat on a cold night.

*Its rural setting is appropriate for this 1950 house as its
antecedents were early nineteenth-century country houses.
This house, in fact, lies in the center of Macon.*

2727 Ingleside Avenue
1950
Sheridan

In 1933, when he was only twenty-four years old, Mr. B. Sanders Walker formed his own real estate firm. Six years later he entered into a partnership with William A. Fickling and then served as president of the Fickling and Walker, Inc. real estate and insurance business for many years thereafter. In 1950 he employed the Ficklings' architect, Harry A. MacEwen, to design a house for his family facing the year-old Fickling house across the valley.

In contrast to the Fickling's Greek Revival style house, the Walker house took the form of a Federal cottage of the early republic, but one which had been added to over time. The mellow old brick of the central portion of the house is complimented by the clapboard-clad extensions of the wings. Mr. MacEwen achieved an artful balance in his design. The central block of the house is formal in its precise symmetry, its dental file molding, and the graceful fanlight in its central pediment. But the formality is relieved by the frame portions, meant to seem like additions, as well as by the use of square columns, rather than round ones, on the portico and by the simple rectangular lights at the entrance door. Overall, he achieved a most pleasing prospect, made even more pleasant by the lush rural aspect of the setting.

Mrs. Walker, Emily, had a keen eye for American antiques, particularly the handcrafted variety fashioned by provincial craftsmen. Over the decades she imbued her home with the look and feel of the early nineteenth century. The spacious, well-appointed rooms were well suited for entertaining large numbers of friends and were arranged for comfortable living for the Walkers and their children.

As the new century began, Lane and Tim Sheridan took possession of her grandparents' house. With the aid of architect Corbin Tucker of Highlands, North Carolina they set about bringing the house up to date. Five rooms that had comprised the kitchen and service area were combined to form a large, open kitchen. The master bedroom was expanded by pushing out two walls by ten feet each. The old garage was demolished and a new, larger one built. The already large family living room was expanded to adjoin a new outdoor living room, patio, and pool. And the attic was converted into a playroom for the couple's two daughters and their friends.

When renovations were complete, Lane and Tim Sheridan had the pleasure of placing back in their rightful places some of the pieces that Emily Walker had chosen for the house. In combination with furnishings that Lane and Tim have chosen, they create a gracious environment to be enjoyed by the Sheridans now and by generations still to come.

Above, The entry hall provides a hearty welcome with its antique sideboard, tall case clock and Persian runner.

At right, A fireplace conversation grouping is but one feature of the very large family room.

At left, Another section of the family room allows casual dining with views to the patio and the woods beyond.

*Family portraits and antique furnishings are
the right appointments in the dining room.*

Above, A view from the formal living room through the entry hall and dining room shows the wide expanse suitable for large-scale entertaining.

At left, The Sheridans expanded the original master bedroom to include a comfortable sitting area.

Entry to this 1956 house designed by Bernard Webb is downhill. Nestled into the hillside, its walls of glass yield views of treetops.

Bernard Alexander Webb, Jr. was in the vanguard of modern architectural design in Macon in the years following World War II. He created more than a score of houses using new principles of design. The houses featured walls of glass to bring the outdoors into the rooms, open floor plans dispensing with doors and, often, with walls, and non-traditional materials such as concrete and plastic. A handful of Webb's houses are truly masterpieces of the style now called Mid-Century Modern. One of these is the house he designed for Dr. and Mrs. Charles Benton.

Charles and Mary Benton were a young couple with small children in 1955 when they started on their adventure of building a house with Bernard Webb. The lot they chose was on a steep hillside where Shirley Hills met the forest. As with many of his clients, Mr. Webb was given free rein by the Bentons to devise a plan for a contemporary house. What he presented to them was bold and innovative. The house could not be seen from the street and only its roof was visible from its own driveway. From a double carport, with a roof of sharp angles, entry was down steps leading to a tunnel-like, roofed, stone walkway enclosed by a wall of the house on one side and a lattice fence on the other. At the end of this tunnel was a carved wood, brightly painted door flanked by glass panels. Inside the door, open spaces flanking the entry extended a total distance of more than sixty feet. Directly ahead, up four steps, was the living room with its angled ceiling sixteen feet high. Its far wall was a plate glass window giving an unobstructed view down a wooded hillside. Similar walls of glass opened the dining room, library, and master bedroom to the outdoors. A long gallery with a translucent ceiling opened onto a large interior courtyard and the master bedroom and bath opened onto their own private walled courts. The kitchen and breakfast room had their own discrete courtyard as well. Access to lower level living space and upper level storage was concealed.

The Bentons were thrilled with their new home and anticipating furnishing these unique interiors and landscaping its several courtyards. Tragically, that did not happen as Dr. Benton was killed in an automobile accident and Mary and her children soon left the remarkable house. One of them, Chris, was so enthralled with the house, and by the building process he had seen, that he became an architect himself and a teacher of architecture at the University of California at Berkeley. Mary later became Mrs. J. Valentino Sheridan and started a long and productive career as one of Macon's leading interior designers.

Over the years the house passed through several hands. By 1998 it was in a sad state of disrepair and had been for sale for eight years. John Waldvogel, a pianist and former teacher, who was disillusioned with life in Florida, came to Macon to look at available real estate. He found the house, fell in love with it and, with the design help of James H. Webb, set about its rehabilitation. The successful collaboration breathed sympathetic new life into this marvelous classic contemporary.

John has furnished the house with a cosmopolitan mixture of furniture enhanced by oriental rugs, exotic accessories, and an art collection including some quite significant pieces. Shortly before his death Mr. Webb and Mary Sheridan visited John, and both enthusiastically congratulated him for his understanding of the house and for making it live again.

A bas-relief of the Chinese goddess Quan-Yin symbolizes the peace and harmony of the interior courtyard.

The entry, library, gallery, and master bedroom all have views into the interior courtyard.

*A lengthy gallery in the center of the house enjoys
light from a glass roof as well as glass walls.*

A pianist, Mr. Waldvogel placed his favorite piano in the living room. It is surrounded by pieces of art from his collection.

*The master bedroom has its own private walled
courtyard.*

The master bath has its own door to the private courtyard.

The architectural firm of Dennis and Dennis designed
this house, one of the first in Idle Hour Estates.

280 Country Club Road
1957
Rogers

Sitting just outside the gates of the Idle Hour Country Club, this classic Georgian Revival house looks as if it might have been transported from Tidewater Virginia or Maryland's Eastern Shore. Credit for its pleasing proportions and its aura of substance belongs to the firm of Dennis and Dennis, Architects. P. E. Dennis started his architectural practice in Macon in 1884. He was eventually joined by his sons, John C. and Ward Dennis. It was 1957 when Mr. Leo B. Huckabee, Jr. asked the long-established firm of Dennis and Dennis to plan a house for him and his family.

Only three years earlier plans had been formed to develop the land bordering the country club, and the real estate firm of Murphey, Taylor, and Ellis had taken charge of selling residential lots. The Huckabees' lot was closest to Idle Hour's entrance and their house was to be one of the earliest built in Country Club Estates. Because of its prominent location and the hope it would encourage others to buy and build in the new subdivision, the house needed to be beyond the ordinary, something to make a statement. Leo Huckabee, called Jack, was confident the Dennises would oblige. He knew something of old family firms, he being a principal of his family concern, the Huckabee Automobile Company, in business in Macon since 1918.

The completed house was a five part Palladian plan. Its central block was fronted with a Greek portico, making it a focal point for the entire composition. The recessed wings, called hyphens, connect with the outer blocks for a harmonious balance. On the interior, rooms were designed for twentieth, rather than eighteenth, century living. A combination kitchen-sitting-breakfast room occupies the rear portion of the center of the house. A master suite takes up the west wing and more bedrooms are in the half-story of the central block. A large general-purpose room is located above the garage, which is incorporated into the east wing.

Mrs. Huckabee, known as "Woo," was an ardent antiques buff who had a great knack for finding just the right piece for just the right place in her house. About the time the house reached perfection the Huckabee children were grown and Jack and Woo decided it was time for a change.

Newlyweds Mr. and Mrs. John F. Rogers, Jr., Jack and Laura, seized the opportunity presented by the Huckabees' decision to move and became the second owners of the house. With period pieces, family heirlooms, and a truly extraordinary art collection, Laura and Jack have made the formal house a comfortable, inviting home. They continue to add to their art collection, always on the lookout for good paintings, particularly those with a nautical theme.

Jack, who enjoys the game of golf, placed his office in a red barn almost on the links so that he can feel he is on the course even when he is working. He hired their Sea Island landscape designer to revamp the grounds. Taking advantage of the tall pines and the stream that meanders through the yard, the designer has enhanced the setting of the house. In the late spring when the hundreds of hydrangeas are in bloom, the Rogers' Dennis and Dennis Georgian house gleams through bowers of pale blue.

The Rogers' family room has a pine paneled fireplace
wall and French doors opening to a patio.

A fireplace and beamed ceiling enrich the breakfast room which opens into the kitchen.

With its fine Doric portico and gracious entry doors, this 1957 house is a Greek Temple dedicated to the gods of hospitality.

1957
Sessions

Stanislaus Circle has as interesting and varied a collection of architecture as any street in Macon. The people who live here are a close-knit group who take pride in their neighborhood. Its original houses date from 1926 when the first lots were sold and the most recent was built in the 1970s. A walk around the circle is a virtual tour of a museum of architectural styles.

The name Stanislaus is taken from the Jesuit College established here in 1874. Originally called Pio Nono for Pope Pius IX and renamed Saint Stanislaus in 1889, the large college building burned in 1921. A priceless library including books four hundred years old was destroyed in the fire. After the fire, the Jesuits sold their property to a real estate development company, which retained the name Stanislaus.

By 1957 few lots were still available on Stanislaus Circle when Mr. and Mrs. Charles Nash purchased this one. Harriett Addams Nash had a talent for improving houses. She bought or built several, lived in them for a time, then sold them and moved on to another. She commissioned an Atlanta architectural firm, Stambaugh and Jett, to design a house for the lot on Stanislaus Circle. What they provided, in collaboration with Harriett Nash, was a Greek Revival house of rare quality. Its dark red brick is accented by crisp white trim and natural stone. Lozenges of a Greek key motif, inset in the architrave, relate its Greek origins. The superb portico is a temple front with columns of the Doric order. Flanking arched niches compliment the double entrance doors. A wrought iron hanging lantern is the perfect accent. Wings that recede from the portico are in proper scale. The combination of elements gives the house a timeless air as if it could have been built a century earlier.

The Nashes lived in the house for several years before selling it to Mr. and Mrs. C. W. Farmer. Charley Farmer was a self-made businessman who owned several successful companies. He and Mrs. Farmer, Erin, had one daughter, June. The couple's favorite flower was the daylily, and they collected innumerable varieties of the flower, some quite exotic, and planted them in beds and borders surrounding the house. In the late spring of each year the Farmers invited people to view the daylilies and attend a party to celebrate their blooming. The daylily party was a Macon tradition.

After Mr. Farmer's death, Mrs. Farmer's health declined and, in 1988, she gave up her house to Mr. and Mrs. J. Brandt Sessions. While planning a total renovation of the house Trudie and Brandt Sessions made every effort to safeguard its architectural integrity. That they succeeded is a tribute to them as well as to the house. The entry hall continues the classical theme of the temple-like portico. Divided by an exquisitely detailed arch, supported by Doric columns and pilasters, it was a special space deserving special treatment. Mary Sheridan and Jean Hogan, of Valentino's Interiors, secured the services of Bob Christian, a Savannah artist who is a master of faux finishes. His elaborately patterned floor of faux marble tiles and walls of faux stone blocks are exactly the right elements for the entrance to a temple. To the left of the entry hall is a large formal drawing room furnished with pieces suited to its fine details. On the right is an equally large and well-detailed sitting room furnished more casually. Beyond it is a bright sun porch outfitted more informally still. At the end of the entry hall is a formal dining room large enough to accommodate family gatherings of the Sessions clan including their two daughters, their husbands, and four grandchildren. The far wall of the dining room is a bow window offering a view of the manicured rear garden. The Sessions converted a carport adjoining the garden into an outdoor living room complete with fireplace. A less noticeable door in the entry hall opens to the bedroom wing of the house. When closed, the door completely separates the family's private quarters from the public part of the house.

Beginning with an elegant but empty shell, Trudie and Brandt Sessions have fashioned a richly appointed but effortlessly comfortable home for themselves. Standing with quiet dignity, their Greek Revival house contributes to the architectural treasury that is Stanislaus Circle.

Above, The central arch dividing the entry hall is supported by Doric columns repeating those on the exterior portico.

At right, The classic theme set on the exterior of the house is continued in the entry hall. Faux artist Bob Christian reinforced the temple concept with the surface finishes.

*The formal parlor is enlivened with
shades of red and rose.*

The sunroom has banks of windows on three walls
providing lots of light for family living.

A portrait of the Sessions' daughter, Parker, introduces a familial note into the large formal dining room.

*This house, designed by Jackson R. Holliday, A.I.A. for
Mr. and Mrs. J. Sewell Elliott, was completed in 1960.*

480 Pierce Avenue
1960
Elliott

This house is still occupied by the couple for whom it was built, Mr. and Mrs. J. Sewell Elliott, Sr. In the late 1950s, Mary and Sewell Elliott needed a house large enough to accommodate their family, which included five young sons. They consulted their close friend, architect Jackson R. Holliday of the Holliday, Couch, Hollis and Jelks firm. Jack had won a reputation for his contemporary designs. But the Elliotts wanted a traditional house. They wanted their friend to design their house and he was anxious to oblige them, and so he was willing to work in an unaccustomed mode.

The property the couple selected on which to build their house was part of the old Winship estate, a tract once measured not in acres but in square miles. As a young girl Mary was taken by her father to play at Slippery Falls, a waterfall on the creek running through the property. Heavily wooded, the property was fairly level near the road but dropped sharply toward the creek behind. The road itself, still fairly rural in aspect in 1960, was named in honor of George Foster Pierce, a Bishop of the Methodist Church and first president of Wesleyan College.

Jack Holliday did an excellent job of siting the house. Taking advantage of the slope, he made the house seem a well-proportioned two stories from the front perspective although it was, in fact, three stories tall. A circular driveway provides a graceful approach to the front door. Inside, an entrance hall discloses an elegant circular stair and leads to a cross hall in the center of the house which gives access to all the principal rooms. The arrangement speaks of the architect's modernist bent and demonstrates that a traditional house can benefit from an unconventional floor plan. At the end of the hall to the left is a large living room with French doors opening onto a gallery overlooking the pool and side garden. Next to the living room is a gentleman's library, and across the center hall from the entry is a spacious dining room with windows overlooking the woods bordering the creek behind the house. The kitchen, family eating area, and service rooms are to the right at the end of the cross hall. The room arrangement makes perfect sense for a large, modern family.

Mary's mother, Mrs. Walter J. Grace, Jr., was from Connecticut. She appreciated early American antiques when such items could still be found outside of museums or Sotheby's showrooms. Mary inherited many of her pieces and needed rooms in which they would feel comfortable. Jack Holliday provided rooms of the proper scale and detail, and Mary Elliott has arranged them with taste and wit. Formal chairs and sofas wear seasonal slipcovers. Family photographs, favorite books, and sentimental bibelots abound. The feeling is one of unplanned elegance devoid of ostentation. All in all, the Elliotts' home seems what it in fact is, a place where generations can gather to enjoy being a family.

This crosshall running through the center of the
house gives access to principal rooms.

American, Oriental, and Victorian antiques are combined artfully in the dining room.

The Elliott's living room extends the depth of the house and opens through French doors onto a second floor balcony.

Taking advantage of a steep natural slope, the house is actually three levels with a second level balcony overlooking the pool area.

1120 Oakcliff Road
1965
Hertwig

Sara Beth Hertwig got a crush on contemporary architecture when she was a student at Agnes Scott College in the early 1950s and dated a student from Georgia Tech's School of Architecture. Her enthusiasm grew after she married Charlie Hertwig from Macon and visited houses designed by Bernard Webb. In 1965, after losing a bidding contest to buy a Webb-designed house, the couple decided to have Mr. Webb design a house specifically for them. Sara Beth found a lot in Shirley Hills but, because it was on an almost vertical slope, she had a hard time persuading her real estate agent to help them buy it. Bernard Webb, however, did not find the lot intimidating. After he had ascertained their requirements, he asked to be left to his "own devices" in designing the house. And, for the most part he was.

What Bernard Webb devised was an Oriental-style house that cascades down the steep hillside. From the road above the house only its wood shake roofs can be seen. Within and without, natural materials, primarily wood and stone, help the house blend into its hillside site. Entry to the house requires crossing a footbridge and stepping into an open stair hall. Beyond is the greatroom with a ceiling that tapers to a central skylight twenty feet above the floor. Large sheets of glass afford views into the surrounding treetops.

Charlie Hertwig, who was initially skeptical about the project, became a convert as the astounding new house took shape. He and Sara Beth set about furnishing it with contemporary furniture, paintings, pottery, and glass. After only five years of enjoying the house, Charlie's employer, The Bibb Manufacturing Company, transferred him to New York and they sold the house. Four years later he was transferred back to Macon, but the house was occupied. The Hertwig's bought a traditional house nearby in Shirley Hills, but kept an eye on the house closest to their hearts. An interim owner was Dr. Raymond Moody, who had gotten national attention with his book recording near death experiences, *Life After Life*. In 1985, Dr. Moody decided to sell the house and the Hertwigs were able to go back home.

During the Hertwigs' twenty-year absence the house had endured alterations not always in keeping with Bernard Webb's plans. Sara Beth and Charlie immediately set about returning the house to its original condition. The specified paint colors were located and re-applied. Landscape designer Martha Duke has created naturalistic gardens to complement the house. Today the house is once again as it was meant to be, the tangible evidence of Sara Beth Hertwig's wishes and Bernard Webb's vision.

*Its site on a steep slope made access by bridge a
logical solution for reaching this unique house.*

*"Like an Oriental Village on a hillside" is one
description for the house and grounds.*

Above, The feel of being in a tree house is stimulated by the ratios of windows to walls.

At right, The house descends its steep slope in a series of levels. Stairs are a dramatic element in its design.

*The soaring ceiling of the living room is brought
to a more intimate level with a stone fireplace.*

*Providing flowers for cutting and herbs for
cooking, this garden is a visual treat.*

1995
Suburban Rivoli

Far out Rivoli Drive, near the old village of Lorraine, stands Macon's last great house of the twentieth century. Being outside the city limits makes the house representative of the continuing trend of outward expansion from the town's center. It is part of Macon although not in Macon. It is indeed a great house in the old meaning of that term—a house of unusual size set among many acres, serviced by accessory buildings and a permanent staff who maintain it. More than that, it is one of the rare houses now being built in the classical tradition, with attention to scale and proportion, suitability of siting, and appropriateness of details.

It is the culmination of a longtime dream of its owners, and of a tedious process as well. The dream was that of a couple who lived for years in a pleasant house in a pretty neighborhood. Their children grew, the husband was successful in business, and the wife was active in the community. Life was good. But they both yearned for something beyond the boxy rooms, low ceilings, and sliding glass doors. The tedious process was the years-long assembling of ideas and analysis of options. Ultimately the process was reduced to three critical questions: what, where, and who. They had a general idea of the house they wanted to build, but were unsure about some specifics. The question of where to build was answered when a large tract of land in a convenient location became available. As to who would design their house, after a long and careful search, they decided on Atlanta architect Norman Askins.

The couple submitted their requirements to Mr. Askins. They wanted space and light, large rooms with tall ceilings, and lots of big windows. The husband wanted a Federal house, the wife an Italian one. Their architect was able to satisfy both by doing what architects have done for centuries—giving the house two façades with different designs.

The dominant feature of the entry façade is a semi-circular portico of classical columns sheltering an entrance door topped by a fanlight with an intricate design in lead. On either side of the covered porch are terraces extending the width of the house. This façade is first viewed through a pecan orchard, beginning at a distance, then circling toward the house to arrive in a cobbled forecourt.

The garden façade pays tribute to Palladio, the sixteenth-century Italian who brought the architectural concepts of ancient Rome to late Renaissance Italy and whose work, *The Four Books of Architecture*, is the foundation of much of western architecture. Centering this façade is a feature often used by Palladio, a recessed loggia with Tuscan columns and a stone balustrade. At either end of the façade are hexagonal bays pierced by tall arched windows. The window design was borrowed, with permission, from the former Eugene O'Neill house at Sea Island. Wide steps lead down from the loggia to a terrace with another stone balustrade.

The loggia and terrace share a vista of a park sloping toward a line of distant trees that appear to recede toward infinity.

A covered walkway on the eastern side of the house is a hyphen connecting the house to a service building and multi-car garage, which are separated by a cobbled motor court. Beside the lattice-walled walkway is a combination kitchen and cutting garden. Visible in the distance under the trees is a special garden, which highlights a statue of the homeowner's great-grandfather in his Confederate uniform. The same soldier's sword was recently found and authenticated and soon will hang in his great-grandson's study.

The interior of the house was carefully and beautifully planned by the architect, the homeowners, and their designer, Dottie Travis of Atlanta. Another of the initial requirements was a hall through the center of the house allowing a sight line from the entrance door through to the garden. The resulting hall is divided into an entry hall on the first level and a stair hall open to the second floor. The circular stair spirals to the upper level without obvious support. The staircase was made off-site and installed in one piece in place. It is a visual poem.

The homeowners have collected fine antiques for many years with the result that the formal rooms are furnished with museum-quality pieces. In the family living room Mr. Askins designed an elaborately patterned ceiling made of pine from a dismantled cotton mill. Mrs. Travis found its seventeenth-century stone mantle in France. The couple enjoys fine wine and in the lower level they installed a tasting room and a high tech room for storage. The antique doors to the wine cellar are of intricately wrought iron backed by glass. In the center of each door was a circular cartouche containing one initial. Unfortunately, it was the wrong initial, so the gentleman of the house had it replaced with his own.

Throughout the house there are interesting architectural features, beautiful things, interesting pieces of art and furniture with fascinating stories associated with all of them. A visit to this great house, again using the old meaning of that term, is a memorable experience. Talking to the couple and sensing their pride in, and enjoyment of, their home is an affirmation that dreams can, and do, come true.

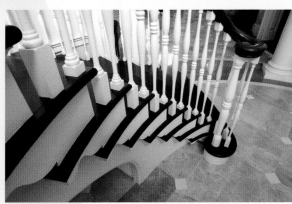

Above, The owners specified that the stair have short risers to allow for comfortable ascents.

At left, The staircase is a work of art gracefully curving upward without visible support.

The central feature of the southern facade of the
house is the loggia, an ages-old Italian concept of
an outdoor living room.

The wine cellar combines antique elements with the most advanced technology for maintaining wine.

Heart pine timber from a Georgia cotton mill was used to create the family room ceiling designed by Norman Askins.

*Connecting the house with the garages, this
passageway is an authentic palladian feature.*